Readings
for
Women's Programs

Second Edition

Edited by
Meg Bowman and Connie Springer

Hot Flash Press
PO Box 21506
San Jose, CA 95151

We acknowledge with heartfelt gratitude the support of the Women & Religion Task Force, a committee of the Pacific Central District of the Unitarian Universalist Association for their encouragement, editorial guidance and support in publishing this book.

Women & Religion Task Force
A Committee of the
Pacific Central District
Unitarian Universalist
Association

Hot Flash Press
Box 21506
San Jose, CA 95151

ISBN 0-940483-00-9

Every effort was been made to trace the ownership of copyright material. If any infringement has been made, apologies are hereby offered, and we will be happy, upon receiving notification, to make proper acknowledgements in future editions. We wish to express our deepest gratitude to all authors who generously extended permissions, and especially to those who allowed alterations and adaptations. We welcome your creativity and urge you to send us material for possible inclusion in a future edition.

CONTENTS

RESPONSIVE READINGS

CIRCLES, CEREMONIES & CELEBRATIONS

SONGS & CHANTS

PREFACE

Hearing a sexist, boring responsive reading one Sunday morning at my church made me angry. "Hell," I said, "I can write one better than that!" As I started writing, I realized that there really wasn't a lot of material about today's women in our rites and rituals. As my consciousness rose and thoughts became written words, I realized that rituals could enhance our feelings of Sisterhood, our sense of "we-ness," as well as denote an opening and a closing for meetings of our local NOW chapter. Then I started lighting a candle and using a responsive reading to mark the opening moment of our Women and Religion Task Force circles, and our Sisterhood grew. The first edition of *Readings for Women's Programs* was published to share these experiences with a larger community.

It has now been twelve years since the first edition of this book was published and, although there have been changes in the status of women, the need for non-sexist rites, readings, and rituals remains strong. In this second edition we have updated some of the material from the first edition and added new material such as, "On Anita Hill and Our Nation's Attitude Toward Women,"by Marianne Neuwirth (page 54) which puts the continuing issues of sexism into a current perspective. This collection, like the first edition, is a gift of love to all wonderful freedom-loving feminists who know that Sisterhood is, indeed, Powerful. We hope that you will find it an effective tool for raising consciousness and enhancing that sense of Powerful Sisterhood.

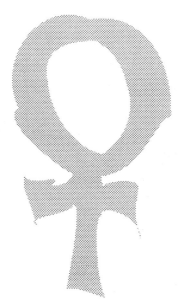

I am convinced that liberation of
women as full-fledged human
beings will prove to be the most
significant expansion of human
rights in the latter part of the
Twentieth Century.

Barbara White
former president, Mills College

Openings & Closings

This section includes readings that are particularly good as openings or closings although many can also be used elsewhere in your program or meeting.

Some are designed as responsive readings and some are readings for one person. Some are specifically openings or specifically closings while others can be used for either.

There are also readings in other sections that can be used as openings or closings. For example, "Candlelighting for Peace and Freedom" on page 111 could be used as an opening ceremony.

Womanspirit Rising
An Opening

We have come from years of pondering

> SILENTLY AND ALONE,
> AS WE NURTURED OUR CHILDREN.

We have come from long, slow generations of women

> WHO KNEW THEIR MIND
> AND WOULD NOT SETTLE.

We have come from the ages of pre-history,
out of the civilizations of Mycenae and Minos,
of Lesbos and Crete.

> OF THE OLMECS AND THE DRUIDS,
> OF MESOPOTAMIA AND CHINA.

We have come through the ages

> BEARING THE CHILDREN,
> NURTURING THE MEN,
> IN SEARCH OF OURSELVES.

We have come to know that

> THE RISING OF THE WOMANSPIRIT
> MEANS THE RISING OF THE RACE.

Now we are discovering and re-discovering ourselves

> AND CREATING AND RE-CREATING
> OUR DEPTHS AND OUR HEIGHTS...

> AND OUR WOMANSPIRIT IS RISING
> AND RISING AGAIN ...

Blessed Be.

From a Unitarian Universalist Women's meeting in Albuquerque, NM

Womanspirit Rising
A Closing

We come to stay forever

> OUR WOMANSPIRIT IS RISING,
> DEEPENING,
> CONVERGING.

We rejoice in it and in one another

> WE WHO ARE MANY ARE ALSO ONE.
> WE WHO ARE ONE ARE ALSO MANY.

On behalf of our Sisters around the globe

> WE GIVE THANKS.

On behalf of our Sisters who have gone before us

> WE GIVE THANKS.

On behalf of our Sisters yet to be born

> WE GIVE THANKS.

We are the past

> AND WE ARE THE FUTURE.

We are the here

> AND WE ARE THE NOW.

We are one, we are Sisters

> AND OUR WOMANSPIRIT IS RISING
> AND RISING AGAIN.

We rejoice in our Sisterhood

> BLESSED BE.

From a Unitarian Universalist Women's meeting in Albuquerque, NM

Sisterhood

We are here

FROM DIFFERENT WORLDS, DIFFERENT LIVES.

Each has lived a different week,

EACH HAS LIVED A DIFFERENT LIFE.

We are unique and different women,

YET WE COME HERE TOGETHER IN SISTERHOOD.

We seek the humanness that is in us all,

WE SEEK THE TRUTH THAT IS IN US ALL.

We seek the understanding that is in us all,

WE SEEK THE LOVE THAT IS IN US ALL.

Blessed Be.

mb

I am not afraid to trust my sisters–not I.

Angelina Grimke
1805-1879

Sisterhood Is Powerful

As we meet together
May we rejoice in our Sisterhood—
    in our singing
    in our listening
    in our thinking together.

Let this hour be bright
    with work and with friendship—
Knowing that we are united;
Knowing that Sisterhood is indeed
    Powerful.

                        mb

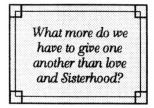

What more do we have to give one another than love and Sisterhood?

Closing Prayer

Goddess, as we journey through the new year*, we are walking into mystery. We face the future, not knowing what the days will bring to us or how we will respond. May love be in us as we journey. May we welcome all who come our way. Deepen our faith to see all of life through your eyes. Fill us with hope and abiding trust that you dwell in us amidst all our joys and sorrows. Goddess, we praise you. Blessed be!

Adapted from "May I Have This Dance?" by Joyce Rupp

* *You can substitute the word "week" or "month" to cover the period between your meetings.*

> *The Goddess of Mercy has a thousand hands, and she needs them all.*
>
> Japanese proverb

Not The First
An Opening

To acknowledge our ancestors means we are aware that we did not make ourselves, that the line stretches all the way back, perhaps, to God; or to gods [or goddesses]. We remember them because it is an easy thing to forget; that we are not the first to suffer, rebel, fight, love, die. The grace with which we embrace life, in spite of the pain, the sorrows, is always a measure of what has gone before.

Alice Walker

A condition of equality for all must exist without regard for differences of sex.

Mary Wollstonecraft
(1759 - 1797)

It Is Enough
A Closing

Even if I am simply one more woman laying one more
brick in the foundation of a new and more humane world,
it is enough to make me rise eagerly from my bed each
morning and face the challenge of breaking the historic
silence that has held women captive for so long.

Judy Chicago

*Great spirits
have always encountered
violent opposition
from mediocre minds.*

Albert Einstein

READINGS

This section contains poems, quotes and stories that can serve a variety of purposes and can be used in a variety of ways. For example, although some of them make good openings or closings we have put them in this section because they are versatile enough to be used in other ways as well. Some could be used as responsive readings and they also work with a single reader. Think flexibility and use them in the ways that work best for you and your group.

Ajar

I stand at the sink
automatically
washing jars.

Absently
I sort out the ones
that are suitable for mixing paint
and washing brushes.

I have not painted in years.

Wash them. Pack them.
Keep track of the lids.
Stack them on the backporch.

I have not painted in years.

Every so often
I need a jar
for cuttings
or taking soup to a friend who is sick.

The cartons of empty jars
move with me
from house to house.

They collect like guilt
in unused corners of the soul.

These jars are not delusions.

They are the humble yearnings
for substance and meaning,
of a heart paralyzed by fear,
desire shelved, disguised.

Every woman saves jars.

Sharon Orr
Artist

'Woman's Play'? Not Today!

Scrub and mop and sweep and clean
(The grass is velvet, shimmering green);
Boil and stew and bake and fry
(White clouds float in a deep blue sky).

Wash and iron and mend and fold
(The sun is turning the air to gold);
Cut and dice and slice and pare
(The scent of lilacs fills the air).

Wax and polish, dust and shine
(A hummingbird's tasting the trumpet vine);
Fit and measure, cut and sew
(The willows sway as the breezes blow).

How I'd love to play in the sun
But a woman's work is never done!

Margaret Pyle Hassert
Wilmington, Delaware

> *Women are still occupied in making the world as the man wants it, and then trying as best they can to create one they can breathe in.*
>
> Anais Nin

Colored Skeins

There is a man who calls me wife
who knows me but does not know my life
and my two sons who call me mother
see me not as any other
yet if the fabric of my day
should be unwound and fall away
what colored skeins would carelessly
unwind where I live secretly?

                                   Mariam Waddington

*A wife is a
silent partner
in someone
else's dreams.*

*In the spring of 1849, the legislature of Tennessee decided that
women had no souls and therefore no right to own property.*

It Is Time

After centuries of self-depreciation
I turn to myself
and smile/

After centuries of self-hatred
I turn to myself
and love/

After centuries of self-doubt
I turn to myself
and trust/

After centuries of silence
I speak/

After centuries of powerlessness
I act/

It is time.

Marieen
Nurse, poet, musician, mother of four,
peace activist from England.

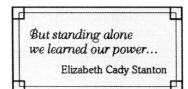

*But standing alone
we learned our power...*

Elizabeth Cady Stanton

"free"

"free"
echoes jubilant
through mind caverns
as men's names used to.

free!
alone on a bus
his grasping love
finally loosed and floating
away in the air like webs.

striding down the street
at my own pace
in my own time
to my own place.

crazy in love
again, this time
with me!

zana

---

*If a woman does not keep pace with her companions,
perhaps it's because she hears a different drummer.*

*Let each step to the music which we hear,
however measured or far away.*

Henry David Thoreau (revised)

Watch Out

Watch out
for that older
woman who once
rocked a cradle
with slippered foot
while humming a simple tune.

She's paid her dues
served her time
now she's ready to move.

An empty vessel sits
on shady shores.
In leaps our woman
with roar and shout,
the broom she holds
becoming an oar
for arms grown strong
through bearing heavy loads.

The water foams,
the water churns,
as she paddles her craft
upstream, forcing that
water to give way.

She sings for joy,
rocking that boat.

Sally Benforado

Coming Out

Well, that was a hard shell to crack —
    But I made it!

Out of the all-too-cozy suburban nest
Out of the middle-aged student hatchery
Out of the stifling, suffocating, smothering,
    mothering, wiving, swiving,
Clutch of marriage!

After 25 years ...

Hey! Look at me! I'm here, world!

I made it!

Coming out — of the house
          of the labor ward
          of the delivery room
          of the class room
          of the closet

I made it! Look at me, world! Here I am!

Does anybody know I'm here?

                              Barbara Glass

---

*The patience of an oppressed people
cannot endure forever.*

                  Martin Luther King, Jr.

Psalm

Blessed is she who has not lingered
in the garden

Her delight is in a new path
She does not walk in the old ways

She is like a young tree
bending beside fresh water

or like a blossom
which bursts full upon a branch

She turns from the man who holds her
from the freedom of the choosing

He is like a keeper of the beasts
who rules with shouts and force

Blest is the day when she shall leave the garden
and the yoke of any man who says
You shall or You shall not

Caryl Porter

That's Why
A reading for two voices

(The two readers speak the underlined lines at the same time.)

Reader 1:	**Reader 2:**

Reader 1:

Because women's work is never done

Or unpaid

Or repetitious.

To get the sack.

Is more important

And if we get raped
It's our fault

And if we get bashed

Provoked it.

And if we raise our voices
We're nagging bitches.

And if we enjoy sex
We're nymphos.

And if we don't
We're frigid.

And if we love women

A "real" man.

And if we ask our doctor

Neurotic

Reader 2:

And is underpaid

Or boring

And we're the first

And what we look like

Than what we do.

It's our fault

We must have
Provoked it.

We're nagging bitches.

We're nymphos.

We're frigid.

It's because we can't get
A "real" man.

Too many questions, we're

Pushy

Reader 1:

Aggressive

Selfish.

And if we expect community
care for children

And if we stand up

Pushy

Unfeminine

Selfish.

And if we don't

Weak females.

And if we want to get married

And if we don't–
We're unnatural.

And because we still can't get

But men can walk on the moon.

Or don't want a pregnancy

About abortion–

And lots

We are part of:
The Women's
Liberation Movement!

Reader 2:

Unfeminine
Selfish.

We're demanding.

For our rights, we're

Neurotic

Aggressive
Selfish.

We're typical
Weak females.

We're out to trap a man.

We're unnatural

Adequate safe contraceptives

And if we can't cope

We're made to feel guilty

And for lots

Of other reasons

The Women's
Liberation Movement!

mb
Adapted from National Union of Students Statement, London

Complacent Women

Complacent women, sitting idly by,
Bestirring not a hand for freedom's sake
Hear you no voices calling you to rise?
Hear you no bitter cries of women slaves,
Scar-marked and cuffed through all the ages past,
The sea dirge of a sea of women's tears?

Complacent women, sitting idly by,
Bereft of dreams, dead-faced, with leaden souls,
What sting will rouse you up to stand erect,
Convert your placid thought to fierce demands,
And warm your hearts with flames of human fire?

Is there within your soul no pride of life,
No whispered music, and no star of hope,
That you have no desire for human rights?
Slaves of ten thousand years, or playthings cheap,
I taunt you, sting you with the tongue of shame,
To rouse you up to claim your heritage.

Max Ehrmann, 1918

If we are not for ourselves -
who will be?
If we are only for ourselves -
of what worth are we?
If not now, when?

Rabbi Hillel
(30 B.C.E. - 9 C.E.)

To Marge Piercy

After surrender
the victor
sets the terms

you wrote

I read that line
against my will
going through
the compromises
of my day

Thinking of Helene
who tries
fitting into
his life
embracing
his goals

We have all
done the
same
each woman
of us

Taught to bend
to put
him first

adaptation
the name
for our surrenders

once taken
we are theirs...

after surrender
the loser
has to pay

the current
him
we learn his
ways

Irene Raby

Millie's Mother's Red Dress
A Reading for Two Women

DAUGHTER:

It hung there in the closet
While she was dying, Mother's red dress,
Like a gash in the row
Of dark, old clothes
She had worn away her life in.

They had called me home,
And I knew when I saw her
She wasn't going to last.

When I saw the dress, I said,
"Why Mother—how beautiful!
I've never seen it on you."

MOTHER:

"I've never worn it,
Sit down, Millie—I'd like to undo
A lesson or two before I go, if I can."

DAUGHTER:

I sat by her bed.
And she sighed a bigger breath
Than I thought she could hold.

MOTHER:

"Now that I'll soon be gone,
I can see some things—
Oh, I taught you good—but
I taught you wrong."

DAUGHTER:

"Mother, whatever do you mean?"

MOTHER:

"Well—I always thought
That a good woman never takes her turn
That she's just for doing for somebody else.
Do here, do there, always keep
Everybody else's wants tended and make sure
Yours are at the bottom of the heap.
Maybe someday you'll get to them,
But of course you never do.
My life was like that—doing for your dad,
Doing for the boys, for your sister, for you."

DAUGHTER:

"You did—everything a mother could."

MOTHER:

"Oh Millie, Millie, it was no good—
For you—for him. Don't you see?
I did you the worst of wrongs.
I asked nothing—for me!

"Your father in the other room,
All stirred up and staring at the walls—
When the doctor told him, he took
It bad—came to my bed and all but shook
The life right out of me. 'You can't die,
Do you hear? What'll become of me?
What'll become of me?'
It'll be hard, all right, when I go.
He can't even find the frying pan, you know.

MOTHER:

"And you children.
I was a free ride for everybody, everywhere.
I was the first one up and the last one down
Seven days out of the week.

"I looked at how some of your brothers treat their wives
And it makes me sick, 'cause it was me
That taught it to them. And they learned
They learned that a woman doesn't
Even exist except to give.
Why, every penny that I could save
Went for your clothes, or your books,
Even when it wasn't necessary.
Can't even remember once when I took
Myself downtown to buy something beautiful—
For me.

"Except for last year when I got that red dress.
I found I had twenty dollars
That wasn't especially spoke for.
I was on my way to pay it extra on the washer.
But somehow—I came home with this big box,
Your father really gave it to me then.
'Where you going to wear a thing like that to—
Soap opera or something?'
And he was right, I guess.
I've never, except in the store,
Put on that dress.

"Oh, Millie—I always thought if you take
Nothing for yourself in this world,
You'd have it all in the next somehow.
I don't believe that anymore.
I think the Lord wants us to have something—
Here—and now.

MOTHER:

> "And I'm telling you, Millie, if some miracle
> Could get me off this bed, you could look
> For a different mother, 'cause I would be one.
> Oh, I passed up my turn so long
> I would hardly know how to take it.
> But I'd learn, Millie.
> I would learn!"

DAUGHTER:

> It hung there in the closet
> While she was dying, Mother's red dress,
> Like a gash in the row
> Of dark, old clothes
> She had worn away her life in.
> Her last words to me were these:

MOTHER:

> "Do me the honor, Millie,
> Of not following in my footsteps,
> Promise me that."

DAUGHTER:

> I promised.
> She caught her breath
> Then Mother took her turn
> In death.

Adapted from "Millie's Mother's Red Dress" by Anita Canfield

See Me

What do you see, nurses, what do you see?
Are you thinking, when you look at me -
A crabby old woman, not very wise,
Uncertain of habit, with far-away eyes,
Who dribbles her food and makes no reply,
When you say in a loud voice, "I do wish you'd try."

Who seems not to notice the things that you do,.
And forever is losing a stocking or shoe.
Who unresisting or not, lets you do as you will,
With bathing and feeding, the long day to fill.

Is that what you're thinking, is that what you see?
Then open your eyes, nurse, you're looking at Me
I'll tell you who I am, as I sit here so still;
As I rise at your bidding, as I eat at your will.

I'm a small child of ten with a father and mother,
Brothers and sisters, who love one another.
A young girl of sixteen with wings on her feet,
Dreaming that soon now a lover she'll meet.
A bride soon at twenty, my heart gives a leap,
Remembering the vows that I promised to keep.
At twenty-five now, I have young of my own,
Who need me to build a secure, happy home
A woman of thirty, my young now grow fast,
Bound to each other with ties that should last.
At forty, my young sons have grown and are gone,
But my man's beside me to see I don't mourn.
At fifty, once more babies play 'round my knee,
Again we know children, my loved one and me.

Dark days are upon me, my husband is dead,
I look at the future, I shudder with dread
For my young are all rearing young of their own,
And I think of the years and love that I've known;
I'm just an old woman now and nature is cruel
'Tis her jest to make old age look like a fool.

The body is crumpled, grace and vigor depart,
There is now a stone where once I had a heart.
But inside this old carcass a young girl still dwells,
And now and again my battered heart swells.

I remember the joys, I remember the pain,
And I'm loving and living life all over again,
I think of the years, all too few - gone too fast,
And accept the stark fact that nothing can last.
So, open your eyes, nurses, open and see,
Not a crabby old woman; look closer, nurses - see Me!

This poem was found among the possessions of an elderly woman
who died in the geriatric ward of a hospital in Oregon.
No information is available concerning who she was or when she died.

> *Ageism is any discrimination against people
> on the basis of chronological age — whether old
> or young. It's responsible for an enormous
> neglect of social resources.*
>
> **Maggie Kuhn**
> **(1905-1995)**

When I Am An Old Woman

When I am an old woman, I shall wear purple
With a red hat, which doesn't go and
            doesn't suit me.
And I shall spend my pension on
            brandy and summer gloves,
And satin sandals, and say we have no
            money for butter.
I shall sit down on the pavement
            when I am tired
And gobble up sample in shops
            and press alarm bells
And run my stick along the public railings
And make up for the sobriety of my youth.
I shall go out in my slippers in the rain
And pick the flowers in other
            people's gardens
And learn to spit.

But maybe I ought to practice a little now?
So people who know me are not too
            shocked and surprised
When suddenly I am old
            and start to wear purple.

Jenny Joseph.

---

*The right to vote, or equal civil rights, may be good demands,
but true emancipation begins neither at the polls nor in courts.
It begins in woman's soul.*

Emma Goldman

Woman To Woman

Woman to woman
Sister to sister
Person to person
We are all cells of one common body of humanity:
Interconnected, inter-related, interdependent,
Of one breath,
Of one earth.
Symbiotically, we need and support each other,
To reach a universal wholeness.
"When my sister weeps, I taste salt."
When she achieves, I rejoice.

As Gaia, in all her autumn beauty
Blends hardwoods, pines and shrubs
With their brilliant burgundies,
Red-oranges, chartreuses and yellows
Into one grand harmony and symphony of color
So she's designed the multi-colored beauty
Of our sisters
Of all races, nations,
Religious and sexual orientations,
Cultures and backgrounds and languages,
Shapes and Sizes—
With equally diverse talents and skills
A rich harvest of cooperation, dedication and POWER.

May our networking and our sense of connectedness
Make us stronger
And even more powerful.
One body,
One unity.

(Let us join hands to feel our oneness...)
Behold a symphony of diversity and color!
Let us celebrate this harvest.
Let us celebrate our unity.
Let us celebrate each other.
Let us celebrate!

So be it.
Blessed be!

Mary Ann Ihm

Mother's Day Proclamation*

Arise, then...women of this day!
Arise, all women who have hearts!
Say firmly:
"Our husbands shall not come to us, reeking of carnage,
For caresses and applause,
Our sons shall not be taken from us to unlearn
All that we have been able to teach them
Of charity, mercy and patience.
We, women of one country,
Will be too tender of those of another country
To allow our sons to be trained to injure theirs."

From the bosom of the devastated earth
A voice goes up with our own,
It says: "Disarm, disarm!
The sword of murder is not the balance of justice."
Blood does not wipe out dishonor,
Nor violence indicate possession.

As men have often forsaken the plough at the summons of war,
Let women now leave all that may be left of home
Let them meet, as women, to bewail and commemorate the dead.
Let them counsel each other as to the means
Whereby the human family can live in peace,...
In the name of womanhood and humanity, I earnestly ask
That all women without limit of nationality,
May join together in
The great and general interests of peace.

*Adapted from "Mother's Day Proclamation"
Julia Ward Howe
Boston, 1870

Patriarchy Defined

Patriarchy is simultaneously the process, structure, and ideology of women's subordination.

Patriarchy is what men do that subordinates or exploits women.

*There can be no free men
until there are free women...*

In education, in marriage, in everything, disappointment is the lot of woman. It shall be the business of my life to deepen this disappointment in every woman's heart until she bows down to it no longer.

Lucy Stone (1855)

What We Did To Win The Vote

On August 26, 1920, when women's right to vote was finally recorded in the U.S. Constitution, Carrie Chapman Catt tallied that it had taken:

- 56 referenda voted on by men

- 277 attempts to get state party conventions to add woman suffrage planks to their platforms

- 480 efforts to get state legislatures to submit suffrage amendments

- 47 campaigns to get state constitutional conventions to write women's suffrage into state constitutions

- 30 concerted drives to get presidential party conventions to make women's suffrage planks a part of national party platforms

- 19 successive lobbying campaigns with 19 successive U.S. Congresses

[Winning the right to vote] cost the women of this country 72 years of pauseless campaigning; millions of dollars were raised...hundreds of women gave the accumulated possibilities of an entire lifetime, thousands gave constant interest, and some did as they could. Young suffragists, who helped forge the last links of that chain, were not born when it began. Old suffragists, who helped forge the first links were dead when it ended.

Carrie Chapman Catt

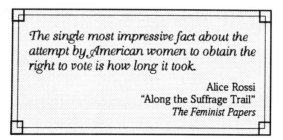

The single most impressive fact about the attempt by American women to obtain the right to vote is how long it took.

Alice Rossi
"Along the Suffrage Trail"
The Feminist Papers

United States Constitutional Amendment 19: Woman's Suffrage

Section 1. The right of citizens of the United States to vote shall not be denied or abridged by the United States or by any state on account of sex.

Section 2. Congress shall have the power to enforce this article by appropriate legislation.

Men their rights, and nothing more:
Women their rights and nothing less

Motto of *The Revolution*,
Susan B. Anthony's paper

Photo © 1992 by C. F. Springer

"The Woman Movement," a sculpture by Adelaide Johnson.
Left to right: Elizabeth Cady Stanton, Susan B. Anthony,
and Lucretia Mott.

Anti-Feminism
A CENTRAL PART OF HITLER'S GERMANY

"The League for the Prevention of the Emancipation of Women"
in Germany was followed by Hitler who ridiculed feminists and
promised if elected to restore male supremacy, disband feminist
organizations and publications, remove feminists from teaching
and other public posts, ban all women from the Reichstag*,
padlock birth control clinics, make abortion a serious crime,
punish homosexuality and ban married women from competing
with men for government jobs. Promising men that women would
soon be relegated to "Children, Cooking, Church" ("Kinder, Kueche,
Kirche"), Hitler instituted all of the above soon after being elected
to power - plus Ravensbruch, a concentration camp exclusively
for women, the site of most Nazi "medical experiments."

Based on "If Hitler Were Alive, Whose Side Would He Be On?"
Outrageous Acts and Everyday Rebellions by Gloria Steinem.
(Holt, Rinehart and Winston, 1983)

* *German legislative body*

---

*In England women are still occasionally used instead of horses
for hauling canal boats, because the labor required to produce
horses and machines is an accurately known quantity, while
that required to maintain the women of the surplus population
is below all calculation.*

Karl Marx in *Capital*, p. 347 (1867)

I Did Not Speak Out

First they came for the Jews
and I did not speak out—
because I was not a Jew.

Then they came for the communists
and I did not speak out—
because I was not a communist.

Then they came for the trade unionists
and I did not speak out—
because I was not a trade unionist.

Then they came for me—
and there was no one left
to speak out for me.

Pastor Niemoeller
German Lutheran Minister

*Behold, how good it
is for sisters to dwell
together in unity.*

Feminist

Profoundly committed
to social change,
not just talk;
a feminist does!
A feminist writes letters,
signs petitions,
organizes marches
and speaks out
on women's concerns –
peace,
equality,
ecology,
health,
day-care centers,
choice.
A feminist works
to "turn the world right side up again;" *
to make the world
a better place.
A feminist is a person who cares.

mb

quoted from Sojourner Truth

Feminism is changing the roots of the soul of the world.

Sonia Johnson

Feminism Defined

feminism: A world-wide social change movement which critically but lovingly rejects relationships and structures based on stereotyped roles of dominance (male) and submission (female).

feminism: A life-affirming movement reorganizing institutions and relationships so that women will have equal access to society's goods, services, status, power.

feminism: The bonding of women discovering the joy of woman-identity.

feminism: A perspective which asks questions such as: Are relationships cooperative or competitive? Are they circular or hierarchical? Inclusive? Interdependent? Can each person participate in those decisions which affect the individual? Can each person be responsible for the communal work? Are all parts of the work valued?

feminism: A process freeing women to work toward liberation for themselves and other oppressed persons.

Roman Catholic Order of Sisters of Loretto
Women's Team

· · · ————◀●▶——— · · ·

fem • i • nism–n. the policy, practice or advocacy of political, economic and social equality for women.

fem • i • nist–adj. or n. an advocate of feminism.

The New Lexicon Webster's Dictionary
Of The English Language, 1989 Edition

· · · ————◀●▶——— · · ·

feminist (n): a) a person who believes that women should have political, economic and social rights equal to those of men.
b) one who believes the implementation of feminist principles will create a more humane type of political power.

Radical Feminist

I call myself a radical feminist, and that means specific things to me. The Etymology of the word 'radical' refers to 'one who goes to the root.' I believe that sexism is the root oppression, the one which, until and unless we uproot it, will continue to put forth the branches of racism, class hatred, ageism, competition, ecological disaster, and economic exploitation.

Robin Morgan

A feminist is a person - man or woman - who understands and wishes to change the injustices of patriarchal systems.

Jane O'Reilly
The Girl I Left Behind (1984)

I myself never have been able to find precisely what feminism is. I only know that people call me feminist whenever I express sentiments that differentiate me from a doormat or a prostitute.

Rebecca West

Feminism is the radical notion that women are people

Cheris Kramarae &
Paula Treichler

Feminism is the greatest spiritual revolution in the history of the world.

Sonia Johnson

Radical

I sit with a
woman
who's left her family
left her husband
left her home
left with nothing
but herself–
herself a bruised woman
beaten by her family
by her husband
by life.
now, bruised and
alone, she sits before me
a free woman laughing.

Amy
Renewal House

Feminism is a conscious and continuous effort to improve the lives of all women, an effort which requires changing the system that defines success merely as making a lot of money.

Jane O'Reilly
The Girl I Left Behind (1984)

---

*What men have to fear most from women is being laughed at.
What women have to fear most from men is being killed.*

Our Commitment

For such a time as this,
We are called to commitment.

For such a time as this,
We are called to struggle.
    Sometimes to listen
    Sometimes to weep
    Sometimes to risk
       or to speak.

Called to be caring,
Called to act,
    For such a time as this.

Adapted from "Women In a Changing World"
National Council of Churches of Kenya
The Economy and Us, (1990), p. 19

*If you are neutral in a situation of injustice,
you have chosen the side of the oppressor.
If an elephant has its foot on the tail of the
mouse, and you say you are neutral, the
mouse will not appreciate your neutrality.*

Desmond Tutu,
1984 Nobel Peace Prize Recipient

The Equal Rights Amendment

Section 1.   Equality of rights under the law shall not be denied or abridged by the United States or by any State on account of sex.

Section 2.   The Congress shall have the power to enforce, by appropriate legislation, the provisions of this article.

Section 3.   This amendment shall take effect two years after the date of ratification.

The E.R.A., written by Alice Paul, was introduced in Congress in 1923 and every successive year until 1972, when it passed. Between 1972 and 1982, a handful of men in three state legislatures prevented the E.R.A. from being ratified as the twenty-seventh amendment to the U.S. Constitution.

[Courage] means having the strength to say 'yes' to conviction, self-reliance or humanity and to say 'no' to injustice, prejudice, and superstition.

Wonder Woman Foundation,
granting 1984 "Woman of Courage" award to Rosa Parks

There Was A Time

There was a time
when you were not
a slave,
           remember that.
You walked alone,
           full of laughter,
you bathed bare-
           bellied.
You may have lost
all recollection of it,
           remember...
You say there are not
words to describe it,
you say it does not
           exist.
But remember,
make an effort
           to remember,
or failing that,
           invent.

                                   Monique Wittig
                                   Les Guerillires

Only women can give to each other a new sense of self.

Women Hold Up Half The Sky

Let us begin a new era
When all humanity
Not half of it
Will join ranks
To conquer the problems facing our world today.
Women hold up half the sky!
Step forward, men,
So that, together, we can hold up
All the sky!

*We must remember that one determined
person can make a significant difference,
and that a small group of determined
people can change the course of history*

Sonia Johnson

Feminist Party Prayer

Hear our humble prayer, O Goddess… for our friends the women, especially for women who are suffering, for all who are over-worked, underpaid, and treated inequitably; for all the wistful women in captivity who beat against their bars; for all who are in pain or dying of boredom in the cages of suburban houses. Help us women to be true friends to women and share the blessings of the merciful; for the same of Thee, our Goddess.

Ah-women

Anonymous

ANONYMOUS was a WOMAN

Our Mother

Our Mother, who art in heaven
Sister shall by thy name.
Our washin's done, our kitchen's clean
On earth—and it isn't heaven.
Give us this day equality
And forgive our shortcomings
As we try to forgive those who have short-changed us.
And lead us **not** into Home Economics,
But deliver us into politics
For there is the power, and the glory and the money
Forever…

Ah-women

Anonymous

Earth Mother

Earth Mother, Who gave us this universe,
Blessed be Thy name.
Beloved be nature.
Beloved be its people.
May we aspire to make this earth our heaven.
And to live in it with simplicity.
Give us what is needed to sustain us;
And lead us not to hurt others,
Nor to destroy our planet,
Or the self-esteem of others.
Allow us to live lives of service
And to care also for ourselves;
For the Earth is our Mother
And She goes on forever.
Blessed Be.

Ann Beaudet

Almighty Isis
A reading for two voices
(The two readers speak the underlined lines at the same time.)

Reader 1:

I am Nature
Ruler of the Elements,

I am ISIS!
Mistress of the Living.

Everlasting

Undying

I, Mother Nature–

Of the sky.

Of the sea.

I am omnipotent!
Respected throughout the world.

The sole manifestation–

Of all gods and goddesses.
I am Mother–

I am called

By many names.
To the Athenians

To those of Cypress Isle

Reader 2:

I am Nature

Progenitor of Worlds,
I am ISIS!

Mistress of the Dead.

Immortal

Eternal.

Control the planets

The helpful winds

I am omnipotent!

Chief of all Deities.

Of all gods and goddesses.

Of all Deities.

By many names.

I am the wise
and valiant Athena

I am Aphrodite or Venus.

Reader 1:

To those of Crete

I AM ISIS!
Immortal

Eternal

To those on the island of Sicily

To the Elusinians*

Or simply Mother of Wheat!
In China

Or Kuan Yin

The Goddess of Mercy
But the Ethiopian people

And those further to the East

More than any others

That are dear to me.

By my true name

ALMIGHTY ISIS!

Reader 2:

I am Artemis or Diana.

I AM ISIS!

Everlasting

Undying

I am called Persephone

I am Mother Demeter
Or simply Mother of Wheat!

I am Nu Qua, the Creator

The Goddess of Mercy.

And those who dwell
in Egypt

Understand my ancient
wisdom

For they know the
ceremonies

And they call me

ALMIGHTY ISIS!

mb
Adapted from Wm. Adlington's 1566 translation of
The Golden Ass by Apuleius

* *Pronounced (EH-LOO'-SIN-IANS)*

Race Of Women

We are a race
of women
That of old
Knew no fear
and feared no
Death
And lived great
Lives and Hoped
great hopes.

Olive Schreiner

Now you have touched the women
You have struck a rock
You have dislodged a boulder
You will be crushed!

Azanian women, South Africa

Create A Human World

Women are too much inclined to follow in the footsteps of men, to try to think as men think, to try to solve the general problems of life as men solve them. The woman is not needed to do man's work. She is not needed to think man's thoughts. Her mission is not to enhance the masculine spirit, but to express the feminine. Hers is not to preserve the man-made world, but to create a human world by the infusion of the feminine element into all of its activities.

Margaret Sanger
(1879-1966)

A woman should not be a mirror image of man's universe. A woman should not try to emulate men, thus taking on masculine traits, she should develop herself, realize herself, gain direct vision into her own being.

Anais Nin

Women may be the one group that grows more radical with age. One day, an army of gray-haired women may quietly take over the earth.

"Why Young Women Are More Conservative", (1979)
Gloria Steinem, *Outrageous Acts and Everyday Rebellions*,
Holt, Rinehart and Winston, 1983

Read Between The Lines

Because I'm a woman I lack something
in HIStory. I've learned of the lands Kings gained
through the glorious end of soldiers' lives,
and how courtly were King Arthur's knights.
And I've read Dante's poems for Beatrice,
and I've read Shakespeare's contemplations on death.
I've learned how Man emerged from a primordial stew,
and how from Man the Hunter Society grew.
Yet despite all this knowledge there's something I'm lacking.
According to HIStory, all women were passive.
Women were silent dolls in courtly games,
and when they had brains they used men's names for pen names.
Women's true History has been repressed,
So I'll search for my heritage in History's silences.

Anonymous

· · · ——◄●►—— · · ·

Half The Population

Women and girls are half the world's population, do two-thirds
of the world's work hours, receive a tenth of the world's
income, and own less than a hundredth of the world's property.*

World Conference, UN
Decade for Women, 1980

*Charlene Spretnak notes, in States of Grace, "According
to the findings presented at the 34th session of the U.N. Commission on
the Status of Women, which ended in March 1990, there has been no tan-
gible progress in achieving real equality for women throughout the world."

Phallic Drift

A compass point always drifts to the North, no matter how you turn the instrument. Phallic Drift is the similar, powerful tendency for public discussion of gender issues to drift, inexorably back to the male point of view.

Phallic Drift is when television coverage of incest concentrates on the injustices done to a few falsely accused male victims, while the masses of genuine (female) victims face invisibility.

Phallic Drift is when the "radical feminists" invited to talk shows are the women who take the "enough already" male-friendly view that the gender wars are won and feminism is already victorious.

Phallic Drift is when female sexual desire is worth discussing only in terms of how it affects, or threatens men.

Phallic Drift is when efforts to combat acquaintance rape are labeled Puritanism, Miss Grundyism, anti-erotic and anti-fun— all code words for taking the male sport out of sex.

Ronni Sandroff in *On The Issues*
1994

• • • ━━━◄•►━━ • • •

Predictability Test

When a boy is born, it is difficult to predict what he will be doing 25 years later. Can you predict with confidence how a girl will be spending her time 25 years later?

Success

She has achieved success who has lived well, laughed often
and loved much; who has enjoyed the trust of other women,
the respect of intelligent men, and the love of children; who
has taken risks and accomplished goals; who will leave the
world a better place than she found it, whether by growing
flowers, writing poems, or helping Sisters; who has appreciated
the beauty of Mother Earth; who has looked for the best in
others, and given others the best in herself; whose life is an
inspiration; whose memory a benediction.

>   Bessie Anderson Stanley, 1904
>   Revised by mb 1995

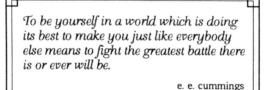

*To be yourself in a world which is doing
its best to make you just like everybody
else means to fight the greatest battle there
is or ever will be.*

e. e. cummings

The Road To Success

To believe in yourself
and in what you can do
Is to take the first step
on the road to success.

*Success is a journey enjoyed,
not a destination fulfilled.*

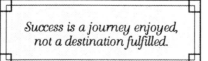

All progress has resulted from people who took unpopular positions.
Adlai E. Stevenson (1900-1965)

A Short Story

The year is 2010.

The President of the United States is a woman. The Supreme Court has eight women and one man. Ninety percent of the House and Senate are women. Men make 59 cents for every $1 that a woman earns.

Men are getting angry. They want to be equal. We women feel they are getting a bit out of hand. Looking back through history, we see that laws that control the human body are an effective means of oppression. We act.

The Supreme Court rules 8 to 1: Ejaculation without the express intent to create life is unconstitutional. The sperm contain half of the genetic material to create life. To ejaculate without intending to create life will be a felony and will carry harsh sentences.

The men in our country are in an uproar. Their cry is heard throughout the nation, "Our bodies, our lives, our right to decide!"

Verna Pitts, 1984

They call us militants, but General Westmoreland, General Abrams, General Motors and General Dynamics — they're the real militants. We don't even have a helicopter.

Florynce R. Kennedy
(Vietnam war era)

On Anita Hill and Our Nation's
Attitude Toward Women

Our nation fears confronting the profound
disrespect and dishonor of women inherent
in our society.

    which is so embedded
       it is not seen as unusual,

    which is present in our daily lives,
       where a woman's image is seen on
          mudflaps and beer bottles,

    which is evident in our actions and words,
       where "he" means everybody,
       and "she" means a storm, or a ship,
          or a nation, or a boat and not
          a fully breathing and thriving
          human being.

    which is present

       in our education,
          where people learn men do great
            things,
          and exceptional women are
            exceptions,

       in history,
          where women are not included,
            except as the mothers of great
              men
            and not the great ones
              themselves,

in religion,
   where we learn men and maleness
      are divine,
   and women and femaleness
      are defiled,
   where Woman caused the fall of
      Man, and still tempts Him
      in evil ways,
   where masculinity and dominion-over
      are revered,
   and the nurturing of, and working
      with the Earth
   are mocked and overshadowed by
      the assertion of "progress"
   which is desecrating our
   Earth,

in advertising, and in movies, and on billboards,
   and on calenders, and on TV,
   where how a woman looks is
   more important than what she does,

in the economy,
   where a woman is told
   she will rise to the top
   by luck or by looks,
   and not by her talent and skill, and
      inherent suitability for the job.
   where women still make only 60% of what
      men make in this country,
      and do not receive equal compensation
         for equal work,

this disrespect and disdain for women goes so deep
as to become ridiculous,
    in that when women cry out against their
        abuse,
    they themselves are put on trial,
    and their character is defamed,
        and dismantled, and they are humiliated
            and subjected to the most ruthless,
                even if subtle,
            kinds of inquisition,
            which can make them
                doubt themselves,
                and their experiences,
                and their feelings,
                and their thoughts,
                and their self-worth,
            and they are seen as
                unusual, or uptight, or self-centered,
                    or man-haters,

and we as a nation, saw clearly
this lack of respect and
lack of honor for women and their experiences in the
Anita Hill/Clarence Thomas hearings

    where Anita Hill's personal integrity was
        rigorously put on trial,

    where there were no black females on the
        panel to validate, invalidate, or
        compare her experience as a blackwoman,

    but was instead filled with white, older
        males, who cannot know a black
        woman's experience,

    where this same panel was witnessed
        to have been more cordial in their questions
            to Clarence Thomas, the accused,
            than to Anita Hill, the accuser,

where the testimony of the witnesses
  stating they had not been sexually
  harassed by Thomas was seen as valid,
  but four witnesses stating an accused
      murderer had not killed them
  would have been dismissed as
      ludicrous immediately,

and because these same women
  and many others
  are so entrenched, enveloped, and
      engulfed by their oppression,
  they collaborate in it fully
      as a well-trained dog who no
          longer needs a leash to obey,
      and like a Bonsai tree whose roots
          are bound by a too-small pot,
          which cripples its growth and
          does not foster it,
      but who feel safe there, and chose
          to stay,
      instead of trying new ground,

and because our nation fears confronting
these abuses against women,
  they perpetuate and proliferate,
  becoming so distorted as to actually
      suggest that women themselves are the
      problem,
  which only supports how deep and
      pervasive
  is this profound disrespect and dishonor
      of women
  and the feminine way.

Marianne Neuwirth
San Jose, CA 1992

My Body

I love my body

For the things it can feel,
For the things it can sense,
For the wondrous things it can do.
For it being alive at the day's beginning
For its weariness at the day's end.

I'm thankful even for its pain,
If only to sting me into awareness
Of my own existence upon Earth

I look upon my body in amazement,
For humans are indeed wonderfully made.
All its secret, silent, complex machinery
Meshing and churning.
What a miraculous design!

I don't want to hurt my body or scar it, or spoil it,
Or overindulge or overdrive it.
But I don't want to coddle it either.
I want to love my body enough to keep it agile
And able and well and strong.

It's the only one I'll ever have.

If you are comfortable with yourself,
You'll be comfortable with others.

Hug One Another

Hugging is practically perfect:
No movable parts
No batteries to wear out
No periodic checkups
Low energy consumption
High energy yield
Inflation proof
Non-fattening
No monthly payments
No insurance premiums
Theft-proof
Non-taxable
Non-polluting
And fully returnable

*Happiness is not
a station you arrive at
but a manner of traveling.*

A hug is worth a thousand words.

The Loving Person

I think the loving person must return to spontaneity–return to touching each other, to holding each other, to smiling at each other, to caring about each other... Hugs are good, they feel nice, and if you don't believe it, try it!

Leo Buscaglia

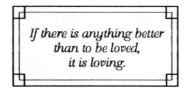

*If there is anything better
than to be loved,
it is loving.*

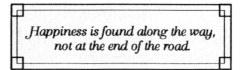

*The real measure of our wealth
is how much we should be worth
if we lost our money.*

J.H. Jowett

*Happiness is found along the way,
not at the end of the road.*

Recipe

1 cup crushed ego
1 teaspoon job discrimination
¼ teaspoon sexual harassment
1 well-beaten path to the washing machine
½ teaspoon grated nerves
1 pinch from a man on the street
1 dash from the dentist to home in heavy traffic
   to release the babysitter

Mix all ingredients together and stir violently. Cool until you
feel a slow burn and then add one last straw. Serves 53% of
the population.

Anonymous

> *It occurred to me when I was 13 and wearing*
> *white gloves and Mary Janes and going to*
> *dancing school, that no one should have to*
> *dance backwards all their lives.*
>
> Jill Ruckelshaus

Yes For My Daughter

It's getting to us, this whole women's lib-
Eration, liberty, the liberal pain:
The surgeon's knife is slicing at the rib
That never quite left Adam. Once again
We're being born, you and I, mother
And daughter. Each of us has stood in a dark
Year and fought the problem for the other—
The problem with no name—that brands the mark
Of battle in our minds.
                    Now worlds of lives
Yawn before us like mouths of giants or bless
With widespread arms of love; which gate gives
Hope? Can each of us alone say yes
To life? Let's practice it as friends who love
Each other; then we can answer when worlds
move.

                                    Jean Embree

*Unless women organize,
support each other, and
force change, nothing basic
is going to happen.*

Gloria Steinem

Women Gathering

Women need to be with each other
In order to affirm ourselves.
It gives us a chance to heal the wounds
    that patriarchy has inflicted upon us.
As we heal, we discover new ways of looking at ourselves,
We find that there is power in being women.
We bring health into our lives.
    and wholeness into our worlds.

Katheleen Weinschenk

I long to speak out the intense inspiration
that comes to me from the lives of strong women.

Ruth Benedict
1917

Stand for Women

Let us confront together...
    confront cruelty
    confront poverty
    confront oppression
    confront fear.

Let us stand together...
    stand for loving
    stand for comforting
    stand for speaking out
    stand for acting
        against corruption
        against violence.

    Stand for women.

                                    Maria
                                    Renewal House

Onward To The Legislature

Onward to the legislature,
To the courts and White House too.
We will take our rightful places,
There is so much we can do.
Use your strength and use
        your wisdom,
Working for the common good.
Let's sing out the song of triumph,
Raise your voice in sisterhood.

Russellyn S. Carruth
Women's Caucus, 1972

*Wherever women gather
together failure is impossible.*

Susan B. Anthony

We Are The Ones

We must remember that we are the ones
we have been waiting for.
We are the ones
who must speak the truth of what we know.
And if we are not healthy,
if we are not filled with the joy of our work,
our voices will be silenced
by our own despair.

Margie Adams

*If you do not express
your own original ideas,
if you do not listen to
your own being, you will
have betrayed yourself.*

Rollo May

Doctor Seuss For Brides

You're going to get married.
Your life will be sweet.
Your dinner won't burn.
Your husband won't cheat.
Your children will come home
With straight A's and then
They'll do all the dishes
And fall asleep at ten.
Your waistline will stay
Perpetually slim.
You'll shop, cook, and clean
With vigor and vim.
But that's in the meantime.
During the day
You'll be on the job
Earning your way.
You won't have to worry
About daycare and such
Your husband does his share
And you're earning so much.
Your medical benefits cover it all.
You'll never get laid off.
You'll never free fall.
The end of the story is
Simple and sweet.
Life for a woman
Is really a treat.

Wallis Leslie

A New Dimension

Our deep concern,
which is so often misunderstood
by women as well as by men,
is not to take over the world
but to assume out fair share
of the burden and responsibility
for the important decisions
which affect all people and our unborn children.

We would add a new dimension of wholeness
which the world has lacked and badly needs.
We must be strong,
for the load is heavy.
We must have courage,
for we face hostility.
We must have stubborn determination,
for we would change attitudes
that have been set for a thousand years.

But let us not sacrifice tenderness,
for the hurting people of the world need love.
With strength let us also be gentle.
Let love enlarge our vision of tomorrow,
and let all bitterness melt into understanding
for all people everywhere.

                                        Polly Laughland

Enraptured

Around her delicate throat
And on her soft breasts
Hung gold necklaces—
Decorated with polished crystals
And small Goddess figurines.

Dancing under the full moon
She wore them proudly.

Around her delicate curls
And down her elegant neck
Glowed red flowers
Bright blue feathers
And multi-colored ribbons.

Dancing under the full moon
She wore them proudly.

Around her sparkling beauty
And the flower-scented air
Radiant moonbeams—gold and blue
Reflected in her hair.

Dancing under the full moon
She wore them proudly.

Blessed Be.

mb
1994

What would happen if one woman told the truth about her life? The world would split open.

Muriel Rukeyser

The women's movement may be, in the long perspective of history, more epoch-making than the fight for racial justice. With the rarest exceptions, women have been subjugated by civilizations of every race and skin color. Their emergence into the light is an event of extra-ordinary significance and– compared to the racial struggle–may ultimately have more far-reaching consequences for human social organizations.

Excerpt from Common Cause Magazine
Sept./Oct. 1984, Vol. 10, No. 5, page 18
An article about John Gradner's book *Excellence*

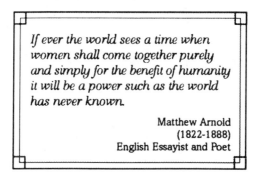

If ever the world sees a time when women shall come together purely and simply for the benefit of humanity it will be a power such as the world has never known.

Matthew Arnold
(1822-1888)
English Essayist and Poet

RESPONSIVE READINGS

Responsive readings usually have two parts. One part can be read by a leader and the other part by the whole group. but they can be done many ways: divide the group into two sections and have each section read a part, have two individuals read the two parts, etc. Do whatever works best for your particular situation.

Responsive readings may be used anywhere in your program. You might use one to "switch gears" from the business portion of a meeting to the program portion. Or you may use one to open or close your meeting or program, to introduce a topic or speaker or to "ground" the group after dealing with a difficult topic.

Anne Hutchinson (1591 - 1643)

Anne Hutchinson arrived with her husband and family
in the Massachusetts Bay Colony in 1634.

WHO ARE YOU, ANNE HUTCHINSON?

I am the daughter of a minister.
I am the mother of 15 children, a midwife and a healer.

AND ARE YOU NOT A DEVIANT WOMAN?

Men gather after church to debate the sermon.
I gather women at my home to do likewise.

YOU LEAD WOMEN INTO SIN.

Wives often develop independent views
from their husbands, and the established church.

THE CHURCH IN THE MASSACHUSETTS BAY COLONY
BELIEVES THE HOLY SPIRIT COMES
ONLY TO THOSE SELECTED BY GRACE.

We women have developed a more generous viewpoint.
We believe the holy spirit is in everyone.

YOU WOMEN DARE TO OPENLY DISAGREE
WITH YOUR HUSBANDS
AND THE CHURCH?

Occasionally, we even walk out of the church.

ANNE HUTCHINSON, WE CHARGE YOU WITH
BEING A HUSBAND RATHER THAN A WIFE,
A PREACHER RATHER THAN A HEARER,
AND A MAGISTRATE RATHER THAN A SUBJECT.

I rely on my intelligence and my intuition:
If this be sin, so be it.

> ANNE HUTHCINSON, YOU ARE EXCOMMUNICATED
> AND BANNED FROM THE COLONY.

My defiant spirit lingers.
Some day women will be church leaders
Some day women will change the world.
Blessed Be

mb

Anne Hutchinson

Mary Dyer

Banished in 1638, thirty-five families followed Anne Hutchinson and her family to Rhode Island. In 1643 they went to the shores of Long Island Sound where Indians who had been defrauded of their land thought she was one of their enemies; she and most of her family were killed.

Twenty years later, Mary Dyer, the one person who had spoken up for her during her long trials, was hanged by the Massachusetts Bay Government, along with two other Quakers, for "rebellion, sedition, and presumptuous obtruding themselves."

Two statues, one of Anne Hutchinson and one of Mary Dyer, stand near the continental center for Unitarian Universalists, 25 Beacon Street, Boston, Massachusetts.

Believe

Believe in who you are

Believe in what is yours.

Believe in your power

> BELIEVE IN WHAT LIES
> IN THE DEPTHS OF YOUR SOUL.

Believe in your strength

> BELIEVE IN YOUR SKILLS
> AND YOUR CAPACITY TO GROW.

Believe in your riches

> BELIEVE IN HEALTH
> AND MOVEMENT AND YOUR BODY.

Believe in your friends

> BELIEVE IN JOY
> AND MIRTH AND SHARING.

Believe in yourself

> BELIEVE THAT YOU ARE STRONG
> AND RICH AND HAPPY.
> BELIEVE IN LOVE
> AND PEACE AND LIFE.

And it will be so.
Blessed Be.

mb

---

*We are what we think. All that we
are arises with our thoughts. With
our thoughts we make the world.*

Buddha

And Then

When women's history becomes part of human history
When both women and men shape the world's future

THEN ALL THAT HAS DIVIDED US WILL MERGE
THEN COMPASSION WILL BE WEDDED TO POWER
AND THEN SOFTNESS WILL COME
TO A WORLD THAT IS HARSH AND UNKIND.

When there is peace and there is good will
When there is equality and there is justice

THEN BOTH MEN AND WOMEN WILL BE GENTLE
THEN BOTH WOMEN AND MEN WILL BE STRONG
AND NO PERSON WILL BE SUBJECT TO ANOTHER'S WILL
AND ALL WILL BE RICH AND FREE AND VARIED.

When the greed of some gives way to the needs of many
When there are new priorities
And new ways to distribute the bountiful harvests

THEN ALL WILL SHARE EQUALLY
THE EARTH'S ABUNDANCE
THEN ALL WILL CARE FOR THE SICK, THE WEAK, THE OLD
AND ALL WILL NOURISH THE YOUNG.

When we all cherish life's creatures

THEN ALL WILL LIVE IN HARMONY
WITH EACH OTHER AND THE EARTH
AND THEN EVERYWHERE WILL BE EDEN AGAIN.

Blessed Be.

mb
Adapted from the last pages of Judy Chicago's
The Dinner Party, A Symbol of Our Heritage
Anchor Books, Doubleday, 1979.

Burnout

Do not burn yourself out. Be as I am. A reluctant enthusiast and part-time crusader.

A HALF-HEARTED FANATIC.

Save the other half of yourself for pleasure and adventure.

ENJOY OUR LOVELY WORLD WHILE IT'S STILL HEAR.

Take a walk or a hike, fish, go on a picnic or a bike ride, mess around with your friends - ramble out yonder and explore the redwoods, climb a mountain, run the rivers, breathe deep of that yet sweet and elusive air.

TAKE TIME TO SMELL THE FLOWERS.

Sit quietly for a while and contemplate the precious stillness of the lovely, mysterious and awesome space.

ENJOY YOURSELF.

Keep your brain in your head and your head firmly attached to the body.

THE BODY HEALTHY, ACTIVE AND ALIVE.

And I promise you this one sweet victory over those desk-bound, up-tight people with their hearts in safe deposit boxes and their eyes hypnotized by their desk calendars.

I PROMISE YOU THIS:

You will outlive the bastards.

mb
Inspired by Edward Abbey

For The Heart That Is Free

For the heart that is free

> LIFE IS A CELEBRATION OF BEAUTY
> A FESTIVAL OF THE SPIRIT.

For the heart that is free

> TIME SHARED WITH FRIENDS BECOMES
> A KALEIDOSCOPE OF PRECIOUS MOMENTS.

Within each of us

> LIES THE POWER TO SEIZE THE HOUR
> AND LIVE BY CHERISHED DREAMS

For the heart that is free

> IS A DELICIOUS GIFT,
> A FRAGILE SAVORED MORSEL.

Each moment a beautiful time

> FOR YOU TO BE YOU
> AND FOR ME TO BE ME.

mb

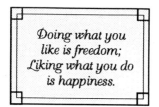

*Doing what you
like is freedom;
Liking what you do
is happiness.*

Just For Today

Just for today
I will try to live through this day only:

    I WILL TACKLE MY PROBLEMS ONE AT A TIME.

Just for today
I will be happy

    I WILL LAUGH.
    I WILL HAVE FUN.

Just for today
I will pet a dog or hold a teddy bear
to feel something soft and fuzzy.

    I WILL TAKE TIME TO SEE THE ROSES AND
    I WILL LISTEN TO MY KIND OF MUSIC.

Just for today
I will strengthen my mind

    I WILL STUDY AND LEARN SOMETHING USEFUL.

Just for today
I will exercise my soul in two ways

    I WILL DO SOMEONE A GOOD TURN
    AND NOT GET FOUND OUT.
    I WILL DO SOMETHING I DON'T WANT TO DO,
    BUT SHOULD DO.

Just for today

    I WILL TELL SOMEONE I LOVE THEM.

Just for today

    I WILL GIVE SOMEONE A HUG.

Just for today
I will have a quiet half-hour all by myself

I WILL RELAX AND TRY TO GET
A BETTER PERSPECTIVE OF MY LIFE.

Just for today
I will be unafraid.
I will enjoy what is beautiful

I WILL BELIEVE THAT AS I GIVE TO THE WORLD,
SO THE WORLD WILL GIVE TO ME.

Blessed Be.

mb
Adapted from Al-Anon

Let Us Praise Famous Women

Let us now praise famous women
Our foremothers who paved the way

> THOSE WHO INITIATED CHANGE
> THOSE WHO LOVED JUSTICE
> THOSE WHO MADE THE WORLD GO.

Let us now praise famous women
Those wise and eloquent teachers
Who steadfastly passed on their culture

> THEIR NURTURING
> THEIR HEALING
> THEIR COUNSEL
> THEIR WISDOM.

Let us now praise famous women
Few were honored in their generation

> BUT THEY LEFT THEIR NAMES BEHIND THEM
> FOR US TO SING THEIR PRAISES.

Let us not sing praises to

> SUSAN B. ANTHONY, ELIZABETH CADY STANTON,*
> ALICE PAUL, MARGARET SANGER, EMMA GOLDMAN
>
> SOJOURNER TRUTH, MARY WOLLSTONECRAFT,
> LUCRETIA MOTT, DOROTHEA DIX, HARRIET TUBMAN.

But most of our foremothers are forgotten

> THEY HAVE NO MEMORIAL
> NO REMEMBERED NAME.
> THEY HAVE PERISHED
> AS THOUGH THEY HAD NEVER BEEN.

* *substitute names appropriate to your program*

All those life-giving women

STRONG, UPPITY, ANGRY, BEAUTIFUL, ABUSED,
RIGHTEOUS, DEPENDENT, ASSERTIVE, COWED AND USED.

With their bodies, most gave birth

AND WE ARE THEIR CHILDREN.
WE SHARE THEIR LEGACIES
FOR WE ARE THE HEIRS
OF ALL THE AGES.

Their bodies are buried

BUT THEY ARE NOT FORGOTTEN
THEIR LIVES SHALL NOT BE BLOTTED OUT.

For we know their wisdom

THEIR FEARS
THEIR DREAMS
THEIR SONGS
THEIR LOVE.

We sing praises to famous women

WE SING THEIR PRAISES
WE SING THEIR PRAISES.

Blessed Be.

mb

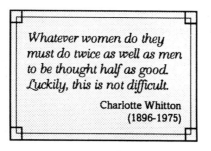

*Whatever women do they
must do twice as well as men
to be thought half as good.
Luckily, this is not difficult.*

**Charlotte Whitton
(1896-1975)**

Praise-Song

Good morning! Good morning!
We praise you, _____(*insert name*)

> YOU ARE LIKE THE MOON AT ITS FULL
> YOU ARE LIKE THE MORNING STAR.

The whole earth is yours

> TO CHERISH AND ENJOY
> MAY YOU ALWAYS BE HAPPY.

You are welcome everywhere;

> WHEN YOU ENTER A ROOM
> JOY IS IN EVERYONE'S EYES.

You are precious. More precious than gold.
We praise you.

> AMONG ALL WOMEN, MAY YOU HAVE A LONG LIFE:
> A LIFE OF DIGNITY AND STRENGTH.

Beat the drum louder!
Louder!

> WE SING, WE SING YOUR PRAISES
> WITH CLEAR VOICES.

And we are happy

> WE PRAISE YOU, _____(*insert name*)
> AND WE HAVE PEACE.

Adaptation of 17th c. West Gumsu
praise-song for female leaders (Africa)

Q Is For Quietness

Q is for quietness
When from steeples everywhere

THE BELLS OF SUNDAY MORNING
RING THEIR QUESTIONS IN THE AIR.

Q is for quietness
When silence walks the city
In her pretty velvet shoes;

WHEN TRUCKS FORGET TO RUMBLE
AND CRICKETS CHIRP THEIR NEWS.

Q is for quietness
On Sunday afternoon...

WHEN WE REST, REFLECT AND PLAN THE FUTURE:
A TIME TO STRETCH AND WALK AND HUM A TUNE.

Q is for quietness
When a child crawls into my lap:

WE ROCK, AND CUDDLE
AND TAKE OUR LITTLE NAP.

Q is for quietness
When I listen to my breathing...

ON SUNDAY MORNINGS, SUNDAY AFTERNOONS
AND DURING THE NIGHT.

And at those special, quiet times...

LIKE...RI G H T NO W

Blessed Be

Inspired by Phyllis McGinley's poem

The Mountain Moving Day

The mountain-moving day is coming.
I say so, yet others doubt.

ONLY A WHILE THE MOUNTAIN SLEEPS.

In the past
All mountains moved in fire.
Yet you may not believe it.

OH MAN, THIS ALONE BELIEVE
ALL SLEEPING WOMEN NOW WILL AWAKE
AND MOVE.

Can you hear the river?
I can see the canyons as they stretch out
for miles.

BUT IF YOU LISTEN YOU CAN HEAR IT BELOW
GRINDING STONES INTO SAND.

Yet you may not hear it.

OH MAN, THIS ALONE HEAR:
THE WATERS NOW
WILL TEAR THE CANYONS DOWN;
THE WATERS NOW
WILL TEAR THE CANYONS DOWN.

The mountain-moving day is coming.
I say so, yet others doubt.

ONLY A WHILE THE MOUNTAIN SLEEPS.

In the past
All mountains moved in fire.
Yet you may not believe it.

OH MAN, THIS ALONE BELIEVE:
ALL SLEEPING WOMEN NOW
WILL AWAKE AND MOVE.

THE MOUNTAIN-MOVING DAY IS COMING.

Yosana Akiko
1911, Japan

A Golden Moment

For a golden moment

  I FEEL AT ONE
  WITH ALL THAT IS.

In a brilliant flash

  I KNOW THAT I AM PART OF ALL
  THAT EVER WAS AND EVER WILL BE.

For a golden moment

  I FEEL AT ONE
  WITH THE GREAT CHAIN OF BEING.

With a glowing radiance

  I REJOICE IN BEING ALIVE
  FOR THIS DAY WILL NEVER COME AGAIN.

For a golden moment

  I FEEL AT PEACE
  WITH MY EARTH
  WITH MY LIFE
  WITH MY SOUL.

  FOR A GOLDEN MOMENT
  I FEEL AT ONE WITH ALL THAT IS.

Blessed Be.

                                             mb

We Are One/We Are Sisters

In Sisterhood, we gather

> REVIEWING THE PAST
> AND DECIDING THE FUTURE.

In Sisterhood, we organize

> GREETING ONE ANOTHER
> WITH WARMTH AND ENTHUSIASM.

In Sisterhood we organize

> CHALLENGING PATRIARCHY,
> THE OLDEST OF INJUSTICES.

In Sisterhood, we share

> BRAVE FOREMOTHERS
> WHO PAVED OUR WAY.

In Sisterhood we raise

> HELL, FUNDS AND OUR CONSCIOUSNESS
> ACCEPTING ONE ANOTHER.

In Sisterhood, we laugh

> AT OURSELVES AND OUR JOKES
> KNOWING THAT LAUGHTER HEALS.

In Sisterhood, we care

> FOR OUR _____ (CHAPTER/RETREAT/CAUCUS...)
> FOR OUR FUTURE
> FOR OURSELVES
> FOR EACH OTHER
> WE ARE ONE. WE ARE SISTERS.

Blessed Be.

mb

Kindling The Light

May the blessing of light be with you always
Light without and light within.
May the sun shine upon you and warm your heart
Until it glows like a great fire
So that others may feel the warmth of it.

AND MAY THE LIGHT OF YOUR EYES
SHINE LIKE TWO CANDLE LIGHTS
IN A WINDOW AT NIGHT
BIDDING THE WANDERER
TO COME IN OUT OF THE DARK
AND THE COLD.

And may the blessings of the rain be upon you,
The sweet and tender rain,
May it fall upon your spirit
As when flowers spring up and fragrance fills the air.

AND MAY THE BLESSINGS
OF THE GREAT RAIN
WASH YOU CLEAN AND FAIR
AND MAY THE STORMS ALWAYS
LEAVE YOU STRONGER AND MORE BEAUTIFUL.

(ALL)
And when the rains are over
May there be clear pools of water
Made beautiful by the radiance of your light,
As when a star shines beautiful in the night
Pointing the way for us all.

Blessed Be.

Celtic/Gaelic translation
from Rev. Robbie Cranch,
Executive Director, P.C.D.,U.U.A.

Self-Love

Self-love is respecting my own uniqueness,
my creativity and my talents.

LEARNING NEW SKILLS,
BEING ASSERTIVE
HAVING CONFIDENCE IN MY ABILITIES

Self-love is acknowledging my good qualities
and following my own guidelines.

SURROUNDING MYSELF WITH PEOPLE
WHO NOURISH ME AND ENHANCE MY SELF-ESTEEM.

Self-love is taking time to enjoy each day.

SURROUNDING MYSELF WITH COLORS AND BEAUTY.
GIVING PLEASURE WITHOUT GUILT.
KNOWING THAT I DESERVE THE BEST.

Self-love is loving and respecting my body.

REALLY TAKING CARE OF MYSELF
PHYSICALLY AND EMOTIONALLY,
GENTLY AND LOVINGLY.

Self-love is seeing myself equal to others,
accepting myself and letting myself win.

NEVER PUNISHING MYSELF
OR HARMING OTHERS.
TURNING MY NEGATIVE THOUGHTS
INTO POSITIVE ONES.

The more I love myself,
the more I can love others
and the more others will return my love.

SELF-LOVE IS
BEING MYSELF
AND ENJOYING MY LIFE.

Blessed Be.

mb

Take Time For 13 Things

1. Take time to dream

    It hitches your soul to the stars.

2. Take time to work

    It is the price of success.

3. Take time to think

    It is the source of power.

4. Take time to play

    It is the secret of youth.

5. Take time to love

    It is the one sacrament of life.

6. Take time to read

    It is the foundation of knowledge.

7. Take time to meditate

IT IS THE HIGHWAY OF REVERENCE
AND WASHES THE DUST OF EARTH
FROM YOUR EYES.

8. Take time to help and to enjoy friends

IT IS THE SOURCE OF HAPPINESS.

9. Take time to make the world a better place

IT IS THE PURPOSE OF LIFE

10. Take time for beauty

IT IS EVERYWHERE IN NATURE.

11. Take time to laugh

IT HELPS LIGHTEN LIFE'S LOADS

12. Take time for health

IT IS THE TRUE TREASURE OF LIFE.

13. Take time to plan

IT'S THE SECRET TO HAVING TIME
TO TAKE TIME FOR THE FIRST 12 THINGS.

mb

Life is what happens to us while we are busy making other plans.

T. LaMance

To Be

BE healthy enough

TO LIVE EACH DAY TO THE FULLEST.

BE strong enough

TO KNOW THAT I CANNOT DO EVERYTHING ALONE.

BE wise enough

TO REALIZE THAT I DON'T KNOW EVERYTHING.

BE courageous enough

TO SPEAK MY MIND AND TO CHANGE MY MIND.

BE understanding enough

TO LISTEN TO THOSE WITH DIFFERING VIEWS.

BE secure enough

TO REVEAL MY OWN UNIQUE PERSONALITY.

BE generous enough

TO ASSIST THOSE WHO NEED MY HELP.

BE frugal enough

TO TAKE CARE OF MY OWN NEEDS.

BE realistic enough

TO FORGET MY PAST AND TO LIVE IN THE PRESENT.

And above all, BE loving enough

TO BE LOVED
TO BE HAPPY
TO BE WHOLE
TO BE MYSELF.

Blessed Be.

mb

To Be Powerful

Marvelous are women's achievements upon this earth.

WE HAVE DISCOVERED OUR STRENGTH,
OUR SKILLS AND OUR POWER.

From preliterate worship of Mother Earth
to the knowledge of many Goddesses

From Healers who knew herbs and magic words
to our foremothers who know how to:

GATHER ROOTS AND PICK BERRIES
PLANT GARDENS AND HARVEST CROPS
COOK MEALS AND CLEAN HOUSES
BAKE BREAD AND SEW CLOTHES

BIRTH BABIES AND NURTURE CHILDREN
FORGIVE BETRAYALS AND MEDIATE CONFLICTS
ORGANIZE WORKERS AND LEAD STRIKES
SING JOYOUSLY AND LOVE HUMANITY

Our skills are many and our power is great.
Marvelous are women's achievements upon this earth.

Blessed Be

mb

With women rest the future of the world.

Voices Of Our Foremothers

We must listen to the voices of our foremothers

CHANTING IN THE MARROW OF OUR BONES.

Men took away our healing and called it medicine

WE MUST RELEARN THE ART OF HEALING.

Then they robbed us of midwifery

AND CALLED IT OBSTETRICS AND GYNECOLOGY.

And with the arrival of twentieth century industrialism

THEY TOOK AWAY OUR MOTHERING
AND CALLED IT CHILD PSYCHOLOGY.

Not only did they rob us, they're making a fortune

FROM OUR STOLEN ARTS
FROM OUR INSECURITIES.

The experts—men—Freud, Spock, Gesell—gave their message
loud and clear: Your son wets the bed? is delinquent? neurotic?

IT'S MOM'S FAULT!
OVER-BEARING/DOTING/REJECTING/WEAK...
NO MATTER WHAT MOTHERS DID, WE LOST.

Our daughters were forgotten in this male-centered psychology.
Then came the women's movement...

WE TOOK BABY-STEPS
TO APPROACH THE REALITY OF OUR RAGE.

How do we repair the damage?

WE MUST LISTEN TO THE VOICES OF OUR FOREMOTHERS
CHANTING IN THE MARROW OF OUR BONES.
WE MUST RELEARN THE JOY OF PARENTING
AND THE MAGIC OF HEALING.
WE MUST TAKE BACK OUR STOLEN ARTS.

Blessed Be

mb
Inspired by "Waking Up The Silence" by Marylou Hadditt
who was inspired by Deirdre English and Barbara Ehrenreich in
For Her Own Good: 150 Years of the Expert's Advice to Women

Together

We have come here today from various places
From seacoasts and deserts; from mountains and valleys
Each with her own thoughts and hopes.

WE COME FROM MANY DIVERSE PATHS OF LIFE
AND YET, WE DO GATHER TOGETHER
WITH SHARED PLANS AND PURPOSES.

And rich we are — a communal repository
of gifts and talents and possibilities.

WE ARE SEASONED AND KNOWLEDGEABLE,
AND, TOO, WE ARE AS VIBRANT AND AS FRESH
AS THE EARLY MORNING.

TOGETHER, each of us seek a common purpose
To effect change in our society, out world.
To carry on the work of our foremothers
For our children's sake and for untold generations to come.

TOGETHER, we come here to create a more just world.
We gather with concerns interwoven into our very being.

We seek peace,
We seek a beautiful environment.

WE SEEK A JUST ECONOMIC SYSTEM,
WE SEEK EQUALITY FOR WOMEN.

We seek racial and ethnic harmony,
We seek that which is good.

FOR PEOPLE,
FOR MOTHER EARTH,
FOR US.

(ALL)
TOGETHER, we are EMPOWERED!
Blessed Be.

We Are Committed

We are women who struggle—

> MANY OF US ARE POOR.
> FROM THE MIDST OF OUR POVERTY
> **WE ARE COMMITTED** TO OVERTURN
> STRUCTURES OF SOCIETY
> THAT BIND US IN A LIFE
> THAT IS LESS THAN WHOLE.

We are women dedicated to change—

> PAID LESS BECAUSE SINGLY
> WE SUCCUMB TO POWERLESSNESS.
> FROM THE MIDST OF THIS INJUSTICE,
> **WE ARE COMMITTED**
> TO ORGANIZE AND STRIVE
> FOR OUR EQUAL WORTH.

We are women from many walks of life—

> OLD
> ALONE
> SINGLE PARENTS
> ILL
> STRUGGLING IN A MALE WORLD.

> FROM THE MIDST OF OUR TEARS OF OPPRESSION
> **WE ARE COMMITTED** TO ESTABLISH HEALTH CARE
> CHILD CARE AND OTHER SERVICES
> THAT WILL EMPOWER US.

We are women struggling to reach our full potential—

> WITHOUT JOBS, ANGERED BY THE INDIGNITY
> OF BEING LAST HIRED AND FIRST FIRED
> FROM THE MIDST OF OUR ANGER
> **WE ARE COMMITTED**
> TO LOOSENING THE CHAINS
> OF STRUCTURAL VIOLENCE
> BY REVOLUTIONIZING THE INHUMANITY
> OF THE MARKETPLACE.

We are women loving women—

> BOUND TOGETHER BY SHARED PAIN
> AND COMPASSION
> FOR ALL WHO SUFFER THE DEGRADATION
> OF POVERTY.

> BOUND TOGETHER BY OUR CONCERN
> FOR ONE ANOTHER,
> KNOWING THAT WHEN ONE SUFFERS,
> WE ALL SUFFER.

> WE NOW PLEDGE OUR TIME, OUR ENERGY,
> OUR INVOLVEMENT.
> WE STRENGTHEN OUR RESOLVE TO BRING ABOUT
> JUSTICE FOR ALL AND
> WE PROUDLY PROCLAIM:

We are women—

> WE ARE POWERFUL
> AND
> **WE ARE COMMITTED!**

Blessed Be.

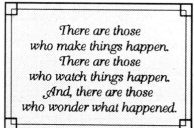

> *There are those*
> *who make things happen.*
> *There are those*
> *who watch things happen.*
> *And, there are those*
> *who wonder what happened.*

To Risk

To laugh

> IS TO RISK APPEARING THE FOOL.

To weep

> IS TO RISK APPEARING SENTIMENTAL.

To reach out for another

> IS TO RISK EXPOSING OUR TRUE SELF.

To place our ideas—our dreams—before the crowd

> IS TO RISK LOSS.

To love

> IS TO RISK NOT BEING LOVED IN RETURN.

To live

> IS TO RISK DYING.

To hope

> IS TO RISK DESPAIR.

To try at all

> IS TO RISK FAILURE.

But risk we must, for the greatest hazard in life

> IS TO RISK NOTHING

The woman who risks nothing

> DOES NOTHING, HAS NOTHING, IS NOTHING.

Anonymous

*Risk is essential.
There is no growth or
inspiration in staying
within what is safe
and comfortable.
Once you find out
what you do best,
why not try
something else?*

Alex Noble

*Risk little.
Win little.*

*Blessed are the risktakers
for they shall acquire wisdom the hard way.*

*Woe unto those who are afraid to take chances
for they shall vegetate.*

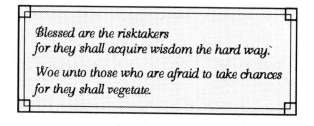

*Life is risk or it
is nothing at all*

Emma Goldman

When I Am Old

When I am old—

> I SHALL WEAR MOSTLY JEANS
> AND T-SHIRTS THAT SAY OUTRAGEOUS THINGS

When I am old—

> I SHALL SPEND MY SOCIAL SECURITY CHECK
> ON CAUSES AND BOOKS
> AND_____* PROGRAMS

When I am old

> I SHALL READ MAD MAGAZINE
> AND PASTE ABORTION ON DEMAND SIGNS
> ALL OVER MY CAR.

When I am old—

> I SHALL PUT COPIES OF THE HUMANIST MANIFESTO
> IN GIDEON BIBLES
> AND TAKE ANTI-DRAFT RESOLUTIONS
> TO THE AMERICAN LEGION CHRISTMAS PARTY
>
> AND MAKE UP FOR THE CAUTION OF MY MIDDLE AGE.

When I am old—

> I SHALL PLANT DAFFODILS IN DITCHES,
> PATRONIZE SERVICE STATIONS WITH PETUNIAS
> AND CONTINUE GETTING BROWN AND WRINKLED
> IN THE SUN.

* *Insert whatever is appropriate, e.g. NOW, WILPF, Unitarian Universalist.*

When I am old—

> I WILL CROSS OUT SEXIST WORDS WITH RED INK
> IN LIBRARY BOOKS
> AND LEAVE PARTIES WHEN SOMEONE TELLS
> A SICK JOKE ON GAYS.

When I am old—

> I WILL SHOOT HOLES IN CHAUVINIST BILLBOARDS
> WITH MY B-B GUN
> AND BE PUSHY ABOUT WOMEN'S RIGHTS.

But for now—

> I MUST NOT SPOIL EVERYONE'S GOOD TIME
> BY GETTING SERIOUS

For now—

> I MUST SMILE PLEASANTLY AT IDIOCY
> AND COMPROMISE TRUTH WITH SILENCE.

For now—

> I MUST NOT OFFEND SOMEONE
> WHO MAY BE IMPORTANT TO MY JOB
> OR MY HUSBAND'S BUSINESS.

But maybe I ought to practice a little now—

> SO PEOPLE WHO KNOW ME
> ARE NOT TOO SHOCKED AND SURPRISED
> WHEN SUDDENLY I AM OLD
> AND START WEARING T-SHIRTS.

From Betty Mill's adaptation of
When I Am An Old Woman by Jenny Joseph.
mb

Wisdom Is A Wise Old Woman

Friends, let us hear the words of Wisdom from ancient times:
Words that have come down to us from the wise old women—

THE CRONE
THE WITCH
THE GODDESS
THE GRAND-MOTHER.

Let us hear their words, that have proved true by the
experiences of all the peoples of the world:

LIVE IN PEACE.
RESPECT NATURE
KNOW THYSELF
LOVE ONE ANOTHER.

Wisdom is learned—

WISDOM MUST BE PASSED ON
GENERATION UNTO GENERATION.

Only those who are foolish ignore the Wisdom of the ages:

FORGET NOT THE LAWS OF RIGHTEOUSNESS—
FOR THEY WILL BRING
PEACE AND SERENITY.

The ways of Wisdom are the ways to happiness
and all Her paths are peaceful—

A LONG LIFE
IS IN HER RIGHT HAND—
IN HER LEFT HAND
ARE HEALTH AND WEALTH.

Wisdom is a wise old woman
And the ways of Wisdom are easy to understand—

> CHOICES AND OPTIONS AND PATHS—
> PONDER EACH, AS YOU FIND YOUR WAY.

Wisdom is a wise old woman
And the value of Wisdom is far above rubies—

> SHE WILL DO YOU GOOD, NOT EVIL,
> ALL THE DAYS OF YOUR LIFE.

Wisdom is a wise old woman,
And strength and honor are Her clothing:

> SHE OPENS HER MOUTH WITH LOVE
> AND IN HER TONGUE IS THE LAW OF KINDNESS.

Wisdom is a wise old woman
And Her children rise up and call Her blessed—

> FOR SHE HEALS THE ILL,
> TEACHES THE IGNORANT,
> CARES FOR THE MOTHERLESS
> AND HONORS PEACE.

So, as you seek your values, your morals, your goals—
As you find your principles, your beliefs, your truths:

> HONOR WISDOM
> OR YOU WILL FLOUNDER
> AND YOU WILL PERISH.

For Wisdom is a wise old woman—
Listen to Her words and be free.
Blessed Be.

                                        mb

We, The People Of The World

We, the people of the world are determined—

> TO SAVE SUCCEEDING GENERATIONS
> FROM THE SCOURGE OF WAR.

We, the people of the world, are determined—

> TO REAFFIRM FAITH IN FUNDAMENTAL
> HUMAN RIGHTS.

We, the people of the world, are determined—

> TO ENSURE THE DIGNITY AND WORTH
> OF THE HUMAN PERSON.

We, the people of the world, are determined—

> TO ENSURE THE EQUAL RIGHTS
> OF WOMEN AND MEN
> OF RICH AND POOR
> THE STRONG AND THE WEAK.

We, the people of the world, are determined—

> TO PROMOTE JUSTICE AND RESPECT
> IN THE RELATIONS OF NATION TO NATION,
> LARGE AND SMALL.

We, the people of the world, are determined—

> TO PROMOTE THE ECONOMIC AND SOCIAL
> ADVANCEMENT OF ALL PEOPLES
>
> TO SECURE THESE ENDS, WE,
> THE PEOPLE OF THE UNITED STATES,
> UNITE WITH ALL PEOPLE OF THE WORLD,
> FOR WE ARE DETERMINED
> TO PUT AN END TO WAR.

World Beyond War

Here on this beautiful planet

THERE IS AN ABUNDANCE OF LIFE.

And among the many species there is humankind

A MIRACLE OF CONSCIOUSNESS
WITH UNDISPUTED DOMINION OVER ALL.

With the human brain

WE HAVE CREATED TECHNOLOGICAL TRIUMPHS.

Unlocking the secrets of the sun and the atom

HAS GIVEN US UNPRECEDENTED POWER
FOR LIFE OR FOR DEATH.

Two paths lie clearly before us:

CONTINUED VIOLENCE AND WAR
UNLEASHED BY FEAR AND HATRED

Or—tolerance, understanding and cooperation

INSPIRED BY A VISION OF A WORLD BEYOND WAR.

The hope for the continuance of life

LIES WITH HUMAN BEINGS
AND OUR ABILITY TO CHANGE THE WAY WE THINK.

We must reach out and find others who share our concern

AND WHO WISH TO BRING ABOUT
A WORLD BEYOND WAR.

Blessed Be.

mb

July 1, 1982—Day Of Infamy

This day will live in infamy.

> THIS DAY THE NATION REFUSED TO RECOGNIZE
> THE EQUALITY OF WOMEN.

This day a handful of male legislators kept the ERA from being ratified.
We are angry, and ours is the rage of women united—

> WHO WILL PASS THE E.R.A.
> WHO WILL WORK FOR PEACE AND EQUALITY
> WHO WILL CHANGE THE WORLD.

Ours is the rage of young mothers
who cannot feed, clothe or educate our children adequately—

> BECAUSE WE HOLD JOBS WHERE EMPLOYERS
> FIND SEXISM COMFORTABLE AND PROFITABLE.

Ours is the rage of our daughters and granddaughters
when they learn that this struggle
which should have been over decades ago—

> MUST NOW SAP THEIR LIFE'S BLOOD
> AS IT HAS SAPPED OURS.

Ours is the rage of millions of women who have been patronized—

> TREATED AS INFERIORS
> AND SHOVED ASIDE TO THE MARGINS OF LIFE.

Ours is the rage of women united—

> WHO WILL PASS THE E.R.A.
> WHO WILL WORK FOR PEACE AND EQUALITY
> WHO WILL CHANGE THE WORLD.

Blessed Be.

mb
Inspired by "This Land Is Stained With The Oppression of Women,"
statement of "a group of women" at the National Archives July 1, 1982.

CIRCLES, CEREMONIES & CELEBRATIONS

This section includes candlelighting ceremonies and readings for women's circles that can be used to add a touch of ritual to your gatherings. They can be used in celebration of a special occasion or to open or close your meeting or program.

Our Ancestors, Our Descendants And Us
A candlelighting ceremony for three readers.

Preparation: *Place three candleholders and a book of matches on a table in the middle of your circle or in front of your audience. Photocopy the ceremony and give three readers their script. No rehearsal is necessary, but be sure readers look at the person who is reading and not down at their script.*

READER 1:

I light this candle for all our courageous foremothers
Who pave the way
Our ancestors who bravely demanded:
An education, the vote, control over their own bodies–
Their womanhood.

READER 2:

I light this candle for our descendants–
Our daughters and their daughters who will follow.
May they have a smoother path–
A life where there is peace, where there is equality,
Where there is love.

READER 3:

I light this candle for us
May we have the strength and the courage,
The self-esteem, self-acceptance, self-reliance, self-love,
Self-honesty and self-confidence
To continue challenging patriarchy– the oldest of injustices*.
Through a bonding of us in Sisterhood,
In love.

mb

Or, challenging injustices wherever we find them.

Touch
A Candlelighting

I light this candle
for all the children—the babies, the infants,
the little people—who have been denied touch;
who have been denied snuggling and cooing
and rocking and kissing and playing and embracing—
the neglected and abandoned—wounded for lack of touch.

I light this candle
for all those who have been harmed by touch—
negative touch.
The battered children, the victims of molest
and incest; the victims of rape and domestic violence.
Those who cry out in their pain.

I light this candle for us.
We who recognize the importance of touch;
we, who touch one another for health,
for nurturing, for caring. We, who hug
and caress one another in a loving way
for we know the joy of touch.

> *Surely the earth can be*
> *saved by all the people*
> *who insist on love.*
>
> Alice Walker

We Are Powerful
Words for a Women's Circle

Directions: *Please hold hands in a circle and, if you wish, close your eyes. I am going to read "We Are Powerful."*

Our hands touch,
We bind together in our womanness.
We touch; we are made whole.
We are made powerful.

Feel your own hidden potentials,
Know your own power.
You can count on me to share the load,
I will be there to help you and to ease your pain.
You can lean on me, I am your sister.
Believe in me, I am your friend.

Our hands touch,
We bind together in our womanness.
Let there be strength, for together
We are powerful.

(This can be followed by three 'om's' and the following:)

In the vision of the Mohawk Chief, Hiawatha—"We bind
ourselves together by taking hold of each other so firmly
that if a tree should fall upon us, it could not shake nor
break our circle, so that our people and our grandchildren
shall remain in the circle of security, peace and happiness."
Our hands touch; we are powerful.

Blessed Be.

mb

Candlelighting For Peace And Freedom

I light this candle for peace

    Peace within our hearts.
    Peace in our homes
    Peace in our communities.
    Peace in our world.

I light this candle for freedom

    Freedom from propaganda and lies.
    Freedom from dictators and repression.
    Freedom from war and bombing and killing and maiming.
    Freedom from oppressive religions and superstitions.
    Freedom from bigotry and hatred—racism, sexism, ageism.

I light this candle for us

    We who gather at this time and at this place.
    We who will spend this hour reviewing our past
    and planning our future.
    We who empower one another to make our lives
    and our planet a better place.

Blessed Be.

Come Into Our Circle

(Leader)
Come into our circle of love and joy
Come into the Sisterhood of justice
Come and you shall know peace
and you shall have love.

Everyone
Raise up your arms and speak out your desires.
Let what you seek for the world penetrate you.
Let truth and kindness pass through you
and you shall know peace
and you shall have love.

Blessed Be

                                        mb

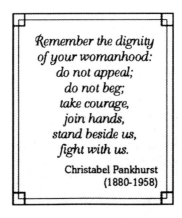

*Remember the dignity
of your womanhood:
do not appeal;
do not beg;
take courage,
join hands,
stand beside us,
fight with us.*

**Christabel Pankhurst
(1880-1958)**

SONGS & CHANTS

Songs and Chants can be energizing and focusing elements of marches, demonstrations and meetings.

They can often be used either in one part, with everyone chanting together or in multiple parts, with separate groups or individuals chanting different sections. In some cases, a leader gives a line and the group "echoes" it back or answers with another line. Some of these chants can be tailored to a specific issue by changing key words. Be creative and use them in whatever way works best for your group or event.

All chants are most effective when repeated several times. The number of repetitions is up to you, but be sure you do enough to feel the rhythm of the chant. Add hand clapping if you want. Have fun!

No More

No more rape
No more war
Violence against women never more!

We All come From The Goddess

We all come from the Goddess
And to her we will return
Like a drop of rain
Flowing back to the ocean.

© Z. Budapest 1971

From You I Receive

From you I receive
To you I give
Together we share
And by this we live.

Joseph & Nathan Segel

No Means No

However we dress,
Wherever we go,
"YES" means YES and
"NO" means NO!

> *One of the reasons that men continue to rape is that they continue to get away with it.*
>
> Susan Brownmiller

I Don't Know ...

I don't know, but I've been told – *(ECHO)*
Womyn's bodies are bought and sold – *(ECHO)*
What I know, and I think I'm right – *(ECHO)*
Womyn have got to take back the night! – *(ECHO)*

Not The Church, Not The State

Not the church,
Not the state
Women must decide their fate

What Do We Want?

What do we want?
Free choice!
When do we want it?
Now!

*No woman will ever be
free until she can choose
whether or not to
become a mother.*

Margaret Sanger
1879-1966

Keep It Safe And Legal

Keep it safe and legal
It's our right
Keep it safe and legal
We will win the fight

Keep it for all women
It's our right
Keep it for all women
We will win the fight

Gentle Angry People

(Repeat many times)
We are gentle angry people
and we are singing, singing for our lives
(or)
We are gentle angry people
and we are marching, marching for our lives.

Morning Has Broken*

Morning has broken
Like the first morning
Women have spoken
Since the first day.
Praise for our vision
Praise for our dreaming
Praise for our courage
In leading the way.

Mine is the sunlight
Mine is the morning
Mine is achieving
All that I can.
Praise for the singing
Praise for the sharing
Let us be equal
Woman and Man.

*Adapted from "Morning is Broken",
words: Eleanor Farjeon,
music: Gaelic melody,
© 1931 Oxford University Press,
harmony by David Evan, 1874-1948

We Are On The Move
To the tune of "We Shall Not Be Moved"

We're marching for all women's lives
We are on the move
We're marching for all women's lives
We are on the move
Just like our mothers fought for rights before us
We are on the move

Demanding reproductive rights
We are on the move
Demanding reproductive rights
We are on the move
Just like our mothers fought for rights before us
We are on the move

Black and white together
We are on the move
Black and white together
We are on the move
Just like our mothers fought for rights before us
We are on the move

Mothers, sisters, daughters
We are on the move
Mothers, sisters, daughters
We are on the move
Just like our mothers fought for rights before us
We are on the move

Abortion, safe and legal
We are on the move
Abortion, safe and legal
We are on the move
Just like our mothers fought for rights before us
We are on the move

Fighting for all women
We are on the move
Fighting for all women
We are on the move
Just like our mothers fought for rights before us
We are on the move

Sisters On A Journey

We are sisters on a journey
Shining in the sun
Shining through the darkest night
The healing has begun
(Repeat)
We are sisters on a journey
Singing now as one
Remembering the ancient ones
The women and the wisdom
(Repeat)

> *Progress is impossible without change;*
> *and those who cannot change their*
> *minds, cannot change anything.*
>
> G.B. Shaw

Hard Is The Fortune

Oh, hard is the fortune of all womankind,
She's always controlled, she's always confined,
Controlled by her parents until she's a wife,
A slave to her husband the rest of her life.

Traditional American Folk Ballad

We Are Dancing Sara's Circle
To the tune of "Jacob's Ladder"

We are dancing Sara's circle,
We are dancing Sara's circle,
We are dancing Sara's circle,
Sisters one and all.

Here we seek and find our history,
Here we seek and find our history,
Here we seek and find our history,
Sisters one and all.

We will all do our own naming,
We will all do our own naming,
We will all do our own naming,
Sisters one and all.

Every round, a generation,
Every round, a generation,
Every round, a generation,
Sisters one and all.

On and on the circle's moving,
On and on the circle's moving,
On and on the circle's moving,
Sisters one and all.

Words by Carole Etzler,
from her album of feminist songs, *Sometimes I Wish.*

Safe And Legal
To the tune of "Frere Jacques"

Safe and legal, safe and legal
It's our right, it's our right
With our banners waving,
We'll continue saving
Women's lives, women's lives.

If men could get pregnant, abortion would be a sacrament.

Florynce R. Kennedy

Keep it Safe and Legal
To the tune of "Buckle Up"

Keep it safe and legal,
It's our right
Keep it safe and legal;
We will win the fight.
Keep it safe and legal,
Stop the hypocrisy.
Keep it safe and legal;
For all women, it's our right.

Battle Hymn of Women
To the tune of "Battle Hymn of the Republic"

Mine eyes have seen the glory of the flame of women's rage
kept smoldering for centuries, burning in this age,
we no longer will be prisoners in the small old gilded cage,
that's why we're marching on.

> CHORUS: MOVE ON OVER OR WE'LL MOVE ON OVER YOU
> MOVE ON OVER OR WE'LL MOVE ON OVER YOU.
> MOVE ON OVER OR WE'LL MOVE ON OVER YOU
> THAT'S WHY WE'RE MARCHING ON.

You have told us to speak softly, to be gentle, and to smile
expected us to change ourselves with every passing style,
said the only work for women was to clean and type and file,
that's why we're marching on.

> CHORUS

It is we who've done your cooking, done your cleaning, kept your rules,
we gave birth to your children, and we taught them in your schools,
we've kept this system running but we're laying down our tools
for we are marchin on.

> CHORUS

You think that you can buy us off with golden wedding rings,
you never pay us half the profit that our labor brings
our anger eats into us, we'll no longer bend to kings,
that's why we're marching on.

> CHORUS

We have broken through our shackles:
Now we sing a battle-song
We march for liberation and we're many thousand strong.
We'll build a new society, we've waited much too long,
now we are marching on.

> CHORUS

There Was a Young Woman
Who Swallowed a Lie

To the tune of "There Was an Old Woman Who Swallowed a Fly"

There was a young woman who swallowed a lie;
We all know why she swallowed that lie.
Perhaps she'll die.

There was a young woman who swallowed a rule:
"Live to serve others"; she learned it in school.
She swallowed the rule to go with the lie;
Perhaps she'll die.

There was a young woman who swallowed some fluff:
Lipstick and blush and powder and puff.
She swallowed the fluff to go with the rule;
She swallowed the rule to go with the lie.
Perhaps she'll die.

There was a young woman who swallowed a pill.
Might have said no but she hadn't the will.
She swallowed the pill to go with the fluff:
She swallowed the fluff to go with the rule;
She swallowed the rule to go with the lie.
Perhaps she'll die.

There was a young woman who swallowed a ring:
Looked like a princess and felt like a thing.
She swallowed a ring to go with the pill.
She swallowed the pill to go with the fluff:
She swallowed the fluff to go with the rule;
She swallowed the rule to go with the lie.
Perhaps she'll die.

One day this young woman woke up and she said,
"I've swallowed so much that I wish I were dead.
Why in the world did I swallow that lie?
Perhaps I'll die."

She ran to her sister; it wasn't too late,
To be liberated, to regurgitate.
She threw up the ring and she threw up the pill;
Threw up the fluff and she threw up the rule.
And last but not least, she threw up the lie.
SHE WILL NOT DIE!

We Are Women

We are the old women
We are the new women
We are the same women
Stronger than before.

We are the flow
We are the ebb
We are the weavers
We are the web.

based on We Are The Flow We Are The Ebb
by Shekninah Mountainwater

I Open My Eyes

I open my eyes to you
I open my heart to you
Together we raise our eyes to the sun
Together we raise our hearts to the sun
And together we are opening
Our loving hearts as one

> *More and more, I begin*
> *to think of a worldwide*
> *Women's Revolution as*
> *the only hope for life on*
> *this planet.*
>
> Robin Morgan
> *Going Too Far*
> (Vintage, 1987)

INDEX

Other Books Available from
HOT FLASH PRESS

Readings for Older Women—Compilation of Wit and Wisdom
Meg Bowman & Diana Haywood, editors.
Essays, poems, quotes and songs that raise consciousness about our ageist
society, help us to feel good about aging and encourage us to do something to
bring about a better world. 311 pages.   ISBN 0-940483-04-1

Feminist Classics: Women's Words That Changed The World
Meg Bowman, editor.
Short articles, book segments, poems and humor from the "Second Wave of
Feminism." 166 pages.   ISBN 0-940483-09-2

Women's History: Dramatic Readings
Meg Bowman
Ideal for classrooms, meetings, or women's history programs. No memorizing.
Readings on Sappho, Hypatia, Mary Wollstonecraft, Deborah Sampson, Emma
Goldman and Elizabeth Gurley Flynn. 225 pages.   ISBN 0-940483-08-4

Goddesses, Witches & The Paradigm Shift
Meg Bowman, editor
More dramatic readings on feminist issues. Includes *Finding Our Foremothers,
Celebrating Ourselves, Three Admirable Women, Four Famous Unitarian Universalist
Women, Bella & Phyllis* as well as *Goddesses, Witches & The Paradigm Shift.*
230 pages.   ISBN 0-940483-03-3

Lilith: Adam's First Wife and Other Dramatic Readings
Meg Bowman
*George Sand: Deviant Extraordinaire; Harriet Ross Tubman; Moon Goddess; Circle
of Sisterhood,* and much more. 235 pages.   ISBN 0-940483-13-0

Memorial Services for Women
Meg Bowman, editor
Material for and by women (or men) of a broad spectrum of beliefs. *"I found
much widom and inspiration...Your insight and unique perception of life have added
to mine"* Leo Buscaglia. 156 pages.   ISBN 0-940483-01-7

Spiral Bound – Collections of Flyers:

Fun Flyers 76 pages.   ISBN 0-940483-06-8
Gross Flyers 77 pages.   ISBN 0-940483-07-6
Silly Flyers 112 pages.   ISBN 0-940483-11-4
Nice Flyers 154 pages.   ISBN 0-940483-14-9
Office Tales 154 pages.   ISBN 0-940483-12-1
Greek Goddesses 60 pages.   ISBN 960-220-623-3

HOT FLASH PRESS
PO BOX 21506
SAN JOSE, CA 95151
(408) 292-1172